PET HEROES

BY NICOLE CORSE

SCHOLASTIC INC.

NEW YORK   TORONTO   LONDON   AUCKLAND
SYDNEY   MEXICO CITY   NEW DELHI   HONG KONG

PHOTO CREDITS
COVER (BOTTOM LEFT): © JEM WILSON/AUSTRALIAN BROADCASTING CORPORATION; (TOP LEFT): © TINA FINEBERG/AP IMAGES; (TOP RIGHT): COURTESY AMERICAN RED CROSS MILE HIGH CHAPTER; (BOTTOM RIGHT): © LORNA ROACH/SPLASH NEWS; BACK COVER: © ANNIE O'NEILL/ PITTSBURGH POST-GAZETTE; P. 1: © LORNA ROACH/SPLASH NEWS; P. 3: © CHRIS CROMER; INSET: © TINA FINEBERG/AP IMAGES; PP. 4–5: © LORNA ROACH/SPLASH NEWS; P. 6: COURTESY OF MARY FLOOD; P. 7: ANITA WESTERVELT/FEMA NEWS PHOTO; PP. 8–9: © SIMON MOSSMAN/EPA/CORBIS; P. 10: © CECIL WHIG/AP IMAGES; P. 11: © TINA FINEBERG/AP IMAGES; P. 12: © RICHARD DICKIN/TRI-CITY HERALD; P. 13: © PAUL ERICKSON/TRI-CITY HERALD; PP. 14–15: JEM WILSON/ AUSTRALIAN BROADCASTING CORPORATION; P. 16: © CHRISTOPHER STARK/LOVELAND REPORTER-HERALD; P. 17: © KMGH, DENVER/AP ARCHIVE; P. 18: © CHRIS CROMER; P. 19: © ROY O'DELL/COURTESY CHRIS CROMER; PP. 20–21: © ANNIE O'NEILL/PITTSBURGH POST-GAZETTE; P. 22: NEWSPIX/ REX USA; P. 23: AUSTRALIAN BROADCASTING CORPORATION/AP ARCHIVE; PP. 24–25: COURTESY AMERICAN RED CROSS MILE HIGH CHAPTER; P. 27: COURTESY MARK CLARK, SCOTTSDALE PD; PP. 28–29: © TINA FINEBERG/AP IMAGES; P. 30: © NATHAN DENETTE/AP IMAGES; P. 31: © COURTESY PURINA-NESTLE CANADA; P. 32: © CHRISTOPHER STARK/LOVELAND REPORTER-HERALD.

DESIGNED BY: MARISSA ASUNCION

ISBN 978-0-545-25837-1

12 11 10 9 8 7 6 5 4 3 2 1   10 11 12 13 14 15/0

PRINTED IN THE U.S.A. 40
FIRST PRINTING, SEPTEMBER 2010

Pets can be great friends and very protective of their owners. But some pets go further than being a good pal. They can perform heroic acts that include saving a person's life or helping another animal. These pets are extra special and can even be called pet heroes.

BONNIE AND CLYDE

Some dogs are trained to help people. They are called service dogs. Guide dogs are a special type of service dog who help blind people. Guide dogs usually lead humans. But Bonnie, a border collie, is an extra-special guide dog.

Clyde

Bonnie

Bonnie

Clyde

She acts as a guide dog for another dog named Clyde, who is blind. Bonnie takes care of Clyde, making sure he can find his food and water. She also takes him for walks.

JAKE

Many people help each other when disasters strike. Some people search for other people while others aid those in need. Jake is a very brave Labrador retriever.

He has helped in many search and rescue efforts, including those after Hurricane Katrina and the September 11, 2001 attacks. Jake has also taught other dogs how to find survivors. That's one courageous canine!

RABBIT

While his owners were sleeping, a bunny named Rabbit smelled smoke. A fire had started in the house. Normally, the smoke detector would have gone off. But the room where the fire started was being painted, and the smoke detector had been removed.

Rabbit's owners were not waking up from the smell, so Rabbit started jumping around and making a lot of noise. He woke up his owners. They were able to escape because of Rabbit's quick actions.

TOBY

When his owner began choking on an apple slice, Toby, a golden retriever, sprang into action. Toby's owner began smacking herself on her chest, trying to move the apple slice, but without any luck.

Toby pushed his owner to the floor and started jumping on her chest. The force of his paws was able to dislodge the apple. His heroic efforts worked and his owner was able to breathe again.

FAITH

Faith, a rottweiler, is a specially trained service dog. Her owner is more likely to have a seizure than most people. Faith is trained to sense when they might happen and to take action. One day her owner fell out of her wheelchair.

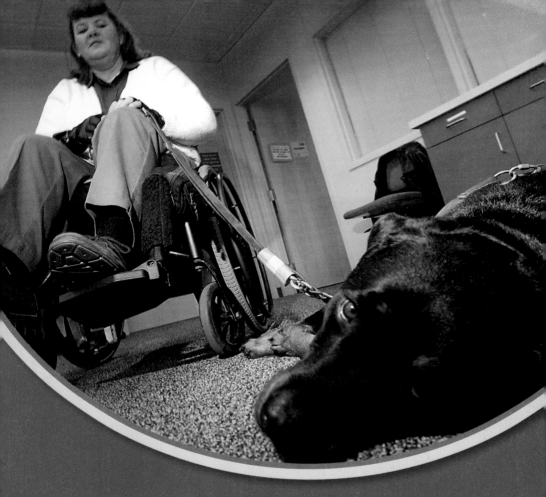

Faith dialed 911 by pressing her nose against the phone. She barked into the phone to alert the person on the other line. She even unlocked the door to let the police inside. Faith's special training saved her owner's life.

PADDY

After retiring from the police force, Paddy, a horse, was living on his owner's farm. One night a brush fire was quickly approaching the house. Soon Paddy's owner's house caught on fire.

Paddy helped protect other animals on the farm by keeping them together in a safe place. Usually animals are scared around fires, but Paddy's background as a police horse helped him remain calm.

ZOEY

A dog is no match for an angry rattlesnake. But don't tell that to Zoey, a Chihuahua. When she saw a rattlesnake lunging toward her owner's one-year-old grandson, she leaped to action without hesitation.

Zoey jumped in front of the child just as the rattlesnake was striking. Instead of biting the child, the rattlesnake bit Zoey. Her face swelled up from the bite, but she survived the attack.

SUZIE

When a man was trapped in the cold mud of a lake, rescuers were called to help. The rescuers knew they had to get a rope to the trapped man to pull him to safety. They also had to give him blankets to keep him warm. And they knew just the dog for the job.

Suzie, a Labrador retriever who has obedience training, was called to the scene and reached the man. Soon the man was pulled to shore. Once Suzie completed her rescue, she sat with the man's son until the man was safely pulled back on land.

LULU

It's hard to believe that a 150-pound potbellied pig could crawl through a doggy door, but that's just what Lulu did to save her owner's life. Lulu's owner was having a heart attack and Lulu knew she needed to get someone's attention, fast.

She climbed through the doggy door and laid down in traffic until someone stopped. Lulu led the person to her owner, and her owner was rushed to the hospital. Lulu risked her life to save her owner's, which makes her a true hero.

LEO

Sometimes cats and dogs do not get along. But Leo, a dog, stayed behind with his family's newborn kittens as a fire burned through his house. Leo waited with the kittens until firefighters arrived to rescue them.

The fire was so strong that Leo and the kittens inhaled a lot of smoke. Luckily, emergency medical responders were able to help them. After they were rescued, Leo gave the kittens lots of kisses. The kittens can thank their friend Leo for his courage.

WILLIE

Some birds can repeat words that their owners say. But Willie, a parrot, added a new word to his vocabulary in an emergency situation. Willie was with his owner while she was babysitting. His owner left the room, and the child she was babysitting began to choke on a piece of food.

In order to get his owner's attention, Willie yelled, "Mama, baby," and flapped his wings. Willie had never said the word "baby" before. Luckily, Willie's owner was able to help the child and Willie became a hero.

BUDDY

It is amazing when a service dog dials 911 to save his or her owner's life. But Buddy, a German shepherd service dog, has called 911 a total of three times! Buddy's owner sometimes has seizures and needs Buddy's help to alert emergency responders. Buddy dials 911 by holding down the buttons on a special phone for more than three seconds with his teeth. Buddy is not only man's best friend—he's also a hero.

WINNIE

Winnie, a cat, is a very loyal pet. One night a carbon monoxide leak started in his house. Winnie knew he needed to wake up his owners in order to save their lives. Winnie climbed into his owners' bed and meowed until they woke up.

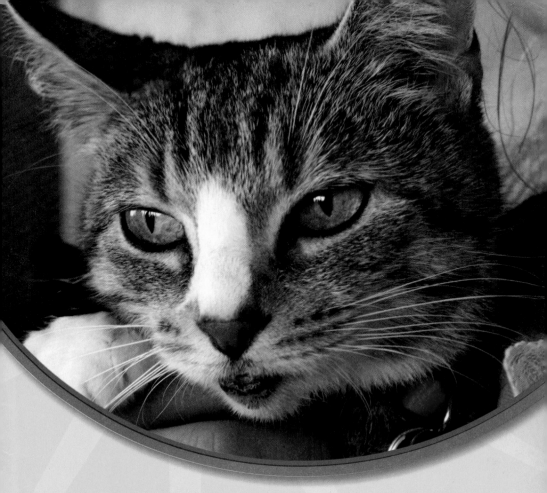

Luckily, Winnie's owners were able to dial 911 and get help before it was too late. After his heroic rescue, Winnie got extra belly rubs and yummy treats from his very thankful owners.

JAROD

Jarod, a chow chow, faced a very scary situation one night in his backyard. Another dog, named Meesha, was outside and encountered a large black bear. Jarod's owner was trying to scare the bear away, but only made the bear angrier.

Jarod rushed out of the safety of his house to protect his owner and Meesha, who were being clawed at by the bear. Jarod eventually scared off the black bear, saving Meesha's and his owner's lives.

Heroes can come in all shapes and sizes. Pet heroes can certainly put their own lives in danger to help others in difficult situations. Whether an animal is a trained service dog or a spur-of-the-moment hero, it is important to treat every animal with love and respect.